DROP-TUNED
RIFF**WRITING**FOR
METALGUITAR

The Creative Guide to Heavy Metal Riff Writing for Drop Tuned Guitar

CHRIS**ZOUPA**

FUNDAMENTAL**CHANGES**

Drop-Tuned Riff Writing for Metal Guitar

The Creative Guide to Heavy Metal Riff Writing for Drop Tuned Guitar

ISBN: 978-1-78933-365-7

Published by **www.fundamental-changes.com**

www.fundamental-changes.com

Join our Facebook Community

www.facebook.com/groups/fundamentalguitar

Instagram: **FundamentalChanges**

For over 350 Free Guitar Lessons with Videos Check Out

www.fundamental-changes.com

Cover Image Copyright: *Artwork for Electric Bears*

Contents

Prologue

For most of life, I've been described as "childish", an advocate of "potty humour", and "a person who constantly daydreams about starring in his own *Teenage Mutant Ninja Turtles* fan fiction stories". Contrary to these hurtful and somewhat accurate pre-adolescent descriptions, I am actually a fully-grown adult in his mid-30s.

Being a gentleman of nearly 35, I've spent 20 years of my life teaching guitar, so I've learned and seen a few things. The catalyst that spawned the idea to create this book was my students constantly asking about overcoming the issue of writer's block, coupled with the familiar sentence, "I've got this one riff… how do I turn it into a song?"

If you're not keeping track, this is my fifth book (yay me!) My previous four books have been based on scales, exercises, theory and how to solo over chord changes. What makes this book so different is that it encourages *you*, the reader, to be creative with building an entire song from the ground up – not as a lead player, but as a composer, creating a song based on solid riffs and chord progressions. There's also some time signature experimentation to keep things interesting.

You might be thinking,

"Chris, you whack man. How you gonna teach me all of that in one book? Gangsta, you be trippin'!"

First, I'd like to suggest you get some elocution and grammar lessons, but also, give me a chance! Throughout this book I'll give you the tools you need to get your riffs and songs happening, including composition assignments and exercises along the way. As you progress through the book, you'll be forced to flex your creative muscles and try things you've never done before.

Writing your own music is, in my experience, the most rewarding part of being a musician. There's only so much emotional and spiritual fulfilment to be had from dedicated scale practice with a metronome and playing covers of someone else's music. Writing music is personal – and it's unique to you, your life experiences, and your quirks as a person and an artist. *Plus*, if you manage to make a living from it, you should definitely high-five yourself. Most importantly, it should make you and the people you are fortunate enough to share it with, happy.

As the title of this book suggests, it is best used by guitarists who want to play Rock and Heavy Metal in drop tuning. From the moment I first heard songs like Rage Against the Machine's *Killing in the Name* and Silverchair's *Freak*, I was hooked on the Drop D sound. Over the years there have been many drop-tuned variants, like tuning down to C#, C or B – you get the idea – but, gradually, drop-tuned Metal and Rock seem to have become the norm, compared to standard tuning.

Of course, you don't have to write Rock and Metal exclusively in drop tuning – it's important to compose in whatever tuning makes you happy and serves your music. But in this book, I wanted to pull together compositional concepts that will ultimately be a useful tool to all the Rock and Metal guitarists of today.

All of the examples in this book are played in Drop D tuning (DADGBE), but they could easily be modulated to Drop C or Drop B. You could even use the concepts shown here on a drop-tuned 7 string, so don't feel like the information presented isn't relevant to you! All the ideas are transferable if you happen prefer a different drop tuning.

You may find some of the composition assignments tricky to get off the ground and organise. Issues can arise with keeping time or filling out bars correctly, especially in Chapter Four, the "odd meters" chapter. I would seriously recommend that you get your hands on the latest version of Guitar Pro, or any reliable guitar tabbing software. This will help you to keep track of your compositions, as well as learning the math behind filling out your meters properly.

I also recommend getting a recording interface if you're able. The Scarlett Focusrite interfaces are relatively inexpensive and do the job incredibly well. I am presently drifting between my Focusrite and my Line 6 Helix Stomp. You'll also need a DAW (digital audio workstation) program like Logic X or Pro Tools. Some people also use Garage Band and Reaper, but in my experience, Logic and Pro Tools have always yielded the best results and sound quality.

But that's enough anecdotal tales of woe and technical jibber-jabber. Let's get excited! Get ready to learn some cool stuff and start writing some music of your very own!

Chris.

Get the Audio

The audio files for this book are available to download for free from **www.fundamental-changes.com.** The link is in the top right-hand corner. Click on the "Guitar" link then simply select this book title from the drop-down menu and follow the instructions to get the audio.

We recommend that you download the files directly to your computer, not to your tablet, and extract them there before adding them to your media library. You can then put them onto your tablet, iPod or burn them to CD. On the download page there are instructions and we also provide technical support via the contact form.

Join our Facebook Community

www.facebook.com/groups/fundamentalguitar

Instagram: **FundamentalChanges**

For over 350 Free Guitar Lessons with Videos Check Out

www.fundamental-changes.com

Chapter One – Riff Writing Foundations

Some of the best songs you've heard grew out of a single riff. A collection of notes that seemingly came out of nowhere went on to set the scene and vibe that would ultimately become the building blocks to create a complete, awesome song.

James Hetfield from Metallica once said that some of their best riffs were created from "noodling on the couch" with an acoustic guitar. Occasionally something sticks out and you go, "Hey, what did I just play? That was kinda cool!"

Not all of us are blessed with "accidental million-dollar couch riffs", frequent surges of artistic inspiration, or daily visits from the muse fairy… but that's normal for the majority of us and there's no shame in admitting it.

In this first chapter we're going to look at how the combination of simple rhythms and a scale can help spawn the creation of a riff.

Common metal rhythms

An 1/8th note is a great place to start when writing riffs. It's a simple rhythm that falls between a 1/16th note (which may be too fast to start with) and a 1/4 note (which may be too slow and rudimentary – so much that you may want to throw your guitar in the bin and take up pottery).

In the first example you'll see a simple 1/8th note rhythm, based around the pedalling open note on the sixth string.

A simple trick to count straight 1/8th notes over a 4/4 bar is "1 & 2 & 3 & 4 &". It may also help to say this counting pattern out loud as you're playing. Try it now.

Example 1a

Once you feel comfortable with this counting idea, move onto Example 1b. Feel free to jam along with the mp3 provided. You can play with alternate picking or strict down strokes if you wish.

Example 1b

Granted, that exercise was offensively basic, but we can zazz it up by changing a few notes to give it a more "riffy" feel.

Play through Example 1c, where I've used the open note as the tonic (D) and switch between the 2nd (E) and the 5th (A) interval.

Example 1c

So far, none of the 1/8th note exercises have had rests, so Example 1d has a simple 1/8th note riff with added rests. These small moments of silence add groove and make an otherwise simple riff less predictable. As cool jazz guys say, "It's the notes you *don't* play."

Example 1d

Next, move on to Example 1e where you'll play through a simple 1/16th rhythm with the open note on the 6th string. With enough practice and metronome drilling, getting an exercise like this tight and effortless will ultimately help bring speed into your riff writing.

A simple trick to counting straight 1/16th notes over a 4/4 bar is,

"1-e-&-a 2-e-&-a 3-e-&-a 4-e-&-a"

Again, it may help to say the counting pattern out aloud as you play this exercise. Another thing to consider is that you'll need to play this with strict alternate picking. It will be too fast to play entirely with down strokes.

The counting pattern and picking directions can be seen in the notation below.

Example 1e

Once this counting idea starts to feel natural, you can move onto Example 1f. It's helpful to jam along with the audio track provided.

Example 1f

In a similar vein to Example 1c, try the next example lick with the added 2nd and 5th intervals, this time using a 1/16th rhythm.

Example 1g

Having played both 1/8th and 1/16th notes in a relatively monotonous and predictable manner, we'll now combine them to create a more interesting metal groove.

The combination of the different subdivisions can make counting and playing the next exercise more challenging. The easiest way to count this eleven-note phrase is to say, "Straw-ber-ry Ice-Cream, Ap-ple-Pie Ap-ple-Pie" for every bar. It's important to note that the varying subdivisions, shifting between 1/8th and 1/16th notes, can wreak havoc on choosing the appropriate picking direction per note, thus the TAB below has every picking direction notated.

Example 1h

When your strawberry ice creams, counting and picking technique are all starting to make sense, move on Example 1i. Here, I've added in some notes on the first three frets to create some interest in between the open ones. Jam along with the audio download.

Example 1i

In a similar vein, the next exercise blends 1/8th and 1/16th notes in a slightly different way. Keep in mind that there are limitless possibilities for creating interesting rhythms in your riffs by doing a simple variance between subdivisions. There's a terrific example of this in the Children of Bodom song *Everytime I Die* at the 0:18 second mark.

The following rhythm differs from all the previous examples, as the rhythmic loop doesn't repeat until two bars have been played. This means our cheeky counting hack (which will no doubt involve food) will span 22 notes across two 4/4 bars. The best way to count these two-barre loops is:

"Co-co-nut Milk, Co-co-nut Milk, Co-co-nut | Milk, Co-co-nut Milk, Ap-ple-Pie Ap-ple-Pie."

See the diagram below and pay close attention to the picking directions.

Example 1j

Now that we have established a counting hack and picking direction, move on to Example 1k and jam along with the mp3. Once again, the first three frets make an appearance in this riff to add some interest and variance.

Example 1k

Having looked at 1/18 and 1/16th note rhythms, let's move on to play consistent triplet 1/8th notes across multiple bars. I always try to give the pulse of my triplet playing a pirate shanty feel. Wag your elbow back and forth like you're on a ship, drinking grog after a lengthy kraken fight.

The easiest way to count triplets is one "Pine-ap-ple" per triplet. In the case of 1/8th note triplets it will be one triplet per beat. You'll also notice that every second triplet has the opposite picking pattern of the previous i.e. the first triplet stroke pattern is notated as "down up down" and the 2nd triplet is "up down up". This means that every bar the 2nd and 4th "Pine-ap-ple" will begin on an upstroke. See the notation below to see the counting method and picking pattern.

Example 1l

Once you've mastered the picking pattern and counting, try Example 1m.

Example 1m

The monotony of playing the same subdivision for multiple bars is not a rule that skips triplets. Too much of ANYTHING can get boring. Using the varying subdivision trick, in the next example I've introduced triplet 1/4 notes to mix up the rhythm and create a more interesting bounce to make the riff groove more. You can hear this being executed perfectly in the Rammstein classic *Keine Lust*.

The next rhythmic idea is two bars in length, with nineteen notes in total before it repeats. It can be counted as:

"Pine-ap-ple, Pine-ap-ple, Cust-ard, Ap-ple | Cust-ard, Ap-ple, Cust-ard, Pine-ap-ple".

See the notation below with counting and picking patterns.

Example 1n

Once this all makes sense, move onto Example 1o. I've put the riff in the key of D Phrygian Dominant to make it more interesting and add more movement.

Example 1o

Using scales on the 6th string to create riff ideas

In the previous section we saw a lot of open notes and only really used the first three frets of the guitar. While this was rudimentary but necessary, it might have felt like a bit of a snooze fest… but not to worry, *insert triumphant raised index finger here* things are about to get a lot more interesting! We're going learn to use scale notes to create more movement and variance in your riffs.

The two scales we'll use for rest of the chapter will be the D Aeolian (Natural Minor) scale and the D Phrygian Dominant scale.

Aeolian is the most common of the minor scales and has a sad melodic quality. The D Phrygian Dominant scale is one of the most used "exotic" scales and is the 5th mode of G Harmonic Minor. To hear more of the Phrygian Dominant scale, check out the band Lamb of God. The song *Laid to Rest* perfectly demonstrates how to use this scale to create riffs. They also have many other songs that are riddled with Phrygian Dominant.

The D Aeolian and D Phrygian scale shapes can be seen in their simplest form in the notation below. I've also included their intervals and note names.

Example 1p

Now play through the entire D Natural minor scale on the 6th string, playing each note four times with an 1/8th note rhythm, as shown below. This exercise will help you begin to play scale notes in a more "riffy" fashion.

Example 1q

Next, you'll play the D minor scale across the 6th string in 3rd interval skips. This immediately sounds less linear and more musical than the previous exercise.

Example 1r

Now play the entire D Phrygian Dominant scale on the 6th string, picking each note four times in 1/8th notes.

Example 1s

This time use a triplet swing rhythm to play through the D Phrygian Dominant scale with skipped 3rd intervals. This is a great way to use the 3rd intervals, with the added bonus of a different rhythmic feel.

Example 1t

Pedalled chugged notes in riffs

This would be a pretty disappointing book if it were just a hundred pages of 6th string riffs. Don't fear! We're about to make a stop in the riffy province known as "Pedal Chug County" (don't Google it, it's not a real place).

First, let's combine an open D drone note with the D Natural Minor scale shape and an 1/8th note pulse. This is where you'll start to see how scale riffs can be written, and get some inspiration and tools to come up with your own.

On a side note, if you wish to do some extra research and listening on this topic, check out the opening riffs in Machine Head's *Aesthetics of Hate* and Testament's classic *Over the Wall* to hear this concept in use.

Example 1u

This simple idea of combining a pedalled open string (or even a fretted root note) with the natural minor scale could literally be used with any scale, as long as it's in key of the pedalling or droning notes.

In the next example you'll combine the D Phrygian Dominant scale shape with a pedalling, open D note and an 1/8th note pulse.

Example 1v

Here's another D Phrygian Dominant riff, this time with the addition of 1/16th notes. This approach will add more chaos, speed and complexity to any riffs you play.

Keep in mind that as you progress through these exercises you'll develop better fretboard knowledge, technique and timing, as well as the ability to switch confidently from one subdivision to the next. Most importantly, you'll start to hear the melodic possibilities that can be spawned from understanding the characteristics and colours of these scales.

Example 1w

Every example of pedalled riffs so far has stayed in one position. However, now you'll work through multiple positions of the of the D Minor scale horizontally across the fretboard.

Example 1x

In a similar vein, the following exercise works through multiple scale positions of the D Phrygian Dominant scale, but this time uses varying subdivisions, jumping between 1/8th and 1/16th notes.

Example 1y

Adding basslines to riffs

So far, each example in this chapter has been based predominantly around an open pedalled note. With too much use this can get a bit predictable, and while it might be charming at first, too many pedalled open note riffs will put a lot of your songs in the same key. But don't fret (no pun intended), with the power of moving basslines we'll have your riffs sounding more colourful and jumping around the fretboard in no time!

Adding a moving bass note infers *chordal movement* and makes the riff move out of zero fret territory.

You might say, "But Chris, how do I infer chordal movement in my riffs? That sounds like crazy smart-guy stuff!" But the idea is quite simple and there is an easy place to start!

When a few bass notes are added, they imply chords from the key centre of the scale you're using.

The table below displays the diatonic chords belonging to the key of D Minor.

Dm	Em7b5	F	Gm	Am	Bb	C
i	ii	bIII	Iv	v	bVI	bVII

First, play through Example 1z, where you'll use a moving bass note to infer chord changes. Pay close attention to the chord numbers referenced in the notation below.

Example 1z

The next example plays through the same bassline and implied chord progression, but this time incorporates more complex rhythms with extensive use of 1/16th notes.

Example 1z1

Here's the D Aeolian scale on both the 6th and 5th strings. The addition of a new string will give you more locations for bass notes in your riffs.

Example 1z2

Next, move on to Example 1z3, where we'll take these scale shapes and play them with a 1/16th note pulse to show you how the bassline scale feels across multiple strings with a faster movement and less monotonous rhythm

Example 1z3

Next, I've used a combination of the two strings to create an implied chord bassline riff with a 1/16th note pulse. I've also added more groove with the incorporation of 1/16th note rests.

Example 1z4

Now it's over to you!

Using these bassline embellishments, complete the unfinished riff below with notes of your own choosing! See how creative you can get with these ideas. Try recording yourself and keeping a diary of your ideas.

There are plenty of assignments in this book and I'd like you to listen to the audio track before trying each one, so you get a good feel for the rhythm and style before launching in. You probably don't want to be rhythm reading right now. Trust your ears, it's more fun!

Example 1z5

The following example uses moving bass notes with position shifting scales to play a cool D Aeolian riff. I've kept the rhythm simple with consistent 1/8th notes.

Example 1z6

In the next few exercises we'll learn how amalgamating a moving bassline with a varying scale shape can be a great tool for riff creation. This approach has been used by many great writers in bands like Trivium, Testament, Killswitch Engage, Machine Head and Eskimo Callboy to name a few.

Let's take a similar approach with the bassline from the D Phrygian Dominant scale on the sixth and fifth strings. This time you'll also play through a few different scale shapes across the fretboard. This will give you bassline/chordal inference options, as well as scale shapes to help you riff around whatever area of the fretboard your bassline takes you.

Example 1z7

Using a combination of moving bass notes and scales shapes using the D Phrygian Dominant scale, I've created an example below that utilises this concept.

Example 1z8

Use the combination of a moving bassline combined with moving scale shapes to compose an 1/8th note riff of your own. Use this incomplete template as a rhythmic guide and place to start. You can always reference (or steal) a few ideas from above!

Example 1z9

The next exercise expands on the ideas shown earlier. This time, however, I've added in some 1/16th notes to make the riff a little more interesting.

Example 1z10

Don't forget, the idea of all these examples is to inspire your own riffs and songs. Please create your own variations and takes on each of them!

Using the same scale structure and format shown in Example 1z7, play through the bassline from the D Aeolian scale on the sixth and fifth string, as well as the different scale shapes shown working horizontally across the fretboard.

Example 1z11

Next, complete the unfinished riff shown in Example 1z12. Replace the dead notes with ones of your own choosing from the bassline and different scale shapes from the D Aeolian scale in Example 1z7.

Example 1z12

Using techniques & expression in riffs

So far, we've covered varying rhythms, moving bass notes and different scale shapes. As a foundation for riff creation, this is a delightful start (if I do say so myself)! But we can make our riffs even more awesome with the addition of some expressive techniques to add flair and variance.

In the next example you'll play through a riff based on the D Aeolian scale on the sixth string. This example shifts between 1/8th and 1/16th notes with the help of some stylish hammer-ons and pull-offs.

Example 1z13

Using the ideas shown above, the next riff uses a moving bassline with a few hammer-ons, but this time also includes slides. This will give the riff a varying approach to how the notes are attacked.

This approach helps break the monotony of every note being picked, but still keeps the 1/16th note pulse consistent.

Example 1z14

Next, play through the D Phrygian scale (mode three of Bb Major) on the sixth and fifth strings using the three different scale positions shown below. This will give you bassline options and a few positions to play scale notes on different strings.

Example 1z15

Using the bassline and the three different one-octave scale shapes, complete the unfinished riff below using notes and techniques (hammers-ons, pull-offs and slides) of your own choosing. See how creative you can get.

Example 1z16

To add 25% more flair to riffs like this and vary them even further, you can add short spurts of speed with 1/16th triplets.

Example 1z17

Eventually you may find the natural minor scale gets a bit predictable. There's a quick trick I use if I'm having writer's block or my riffs are sounding too "samey". The premise is to take a pre-existing riff, but re-imagine it in a different mode. Let's try a similar idea but use the D Lydian mode instead.

The Lydian sound is synonymous with dreamy sounding or galactic "spacey" sounding music, as well as being frequently used by Steve Vai, Joe Satriani and prog metal legends Dream Theater. Below is the D Lydian scale in one octave in its most basic form and also in a one-string format for bassline reference.

Example 1z18

In this riff example I reuse a riff vibe and triplet emphasis from earlier, but with D Lydian instead of Aeolian.

Example 1z19

Using similar emphasis and techniques, create your own riff using the template below. Use either D Phrygian, Phrygian Dominant, Aeolian or Lydian modes. Replace all sixth string dead notes with bass notes and the others with scale notes from the octave shapes shown previously.

Example 1z20

Any of the concepts shown throughout this chapter could be applied using Harmonic Minor, Phrygian, Phrygian Dominant, Lydian Dominant or Locrian scales to name a few. The possibilities are endless.

At the end of day, it's all about your tastes and preferences, and your ability to experiment until you find the sounds you're looking for.

See how far you can take these ideas. Change the order of chords, notes, rhythms, accents and mutes... see what you can come up with! The sky's the limit.

Chapter Two – Chord Progression Writing Basics

A cool riff can sometimes fall out of nowhere and get you super excited about playing, recording and sharing this new snippet of music with the band and fans. However, many of us end up with a bunch of riffs that never properly evolved into fully realised songs, as writing a follow-up section had us stumped. Otherwise known as writer's block!

My opinion is that writer's block can often be attributed to two things: laziness or simply not understanding what options are available to you as a composer. In fact, with the right tools you can quickly turn "a couple of riffs" into a well-written, well-crafted song.

As cool as a great riff is, it is nothing without a well thought out song structure and chords. These ultimately become the foundation for vocal melody and storytelling.

Chords are an important part of all this, so before we get into any of the fun stuff, it's important that we get our definition of a "chord" correct, so that we're all on the same page.

Diatonic power chords in drop tuning

Using drop tuning isn't just about playing so low that only whales can hear you (yes, I'm talking to you, Meshuggah!) For me, it's about the unique tones that are created when distorted heavy chords are played, along with easy construction on the guitar and their ability to be extended.

We'll begin by examining the most common chord used in rock: the humble yet triumphant *power chord*.

A power chord is the combination of a root note and a perfect 5th interval. As it doesn't contain a characteristic 3rd, it has no obvious melodic or emotive definition and is written as simply a "5" chord. For example, E5.

Let's play through the D Natural Minor scale using diatonic power chords. Notice that the second chord is an E5(b5). Check out the opening of Opeth's masterpiece *Heir Apparent* to hear this magical, tense, evil chord in action!

Other than chord ii, all the power chords in drop tuning can be played with a barre across the strings. Handy!

Example 2a

Play through the chord progression written below. I've kept the rhythm nice and simple with varying emphasis on palm muted and regular and/or unmuted notes.

Bars three and four are the same as bars seven and eight. I just wanted to show the different ways you could play the same chord. Having options can change the way you write a chord progression or the way a song flows on the guitar.

Example 2b

Use the chords from Example 2a and the chord progression above to play through the assignment below to fill out the dead notes with a chord progression of your own.

Example 2c

Now would be a good time to start exploring as many drop-tuned power chord sequences as you can. Jam for a while and see what you can come up with before moving on to the next section. Try varying the order of chords, the articulations and where you palm mute. Has some fun exploring the guitar!

Diatonic triads in drop tuning

The last five decades of rock, punk and metal have mainly been kept afloat by the humble, versatile and incredibly useful power chord.

Not to be elitist, but as your palette begins to mature, sometimes the "meat & veg" power chord just doesn't cut it. Your ears will start to hear more complex chords, without knowing how to apply them. A good place to start exploring these sounds is to turn our power chords into triads.

The addition of a major or minor 3rd turns a power chord into a major or minor triad, giving the chord more emotional depth. It goes from being neutral to having enough melodic definition for the listen to determine whether it sounds happy or sad.

To do this, all we need to do is add the 3rd to the top of the chord, as can be seen in multiple songs from bands like Trivium, Slipknot and Opeth to name a few.

Play through the diatonic chord progression in E Minor shown below.

Sidenote: I've replaced the second chord of the sequence with a D/F# (instead of the diatonic Dmb5) as I think it sounds better in this context.

Example 2d

Next, I've combined 1/8th and 1/16th rhythms to create a chord progression in E Minor, using the new drop-tuned triads.

Example 2e

Now combine the diatonic triad shapes with the rhythms and stylistic approaches shown above to fill out the unfinished template below. Replace the dead notes with triad chords from E Minor to create your own chord progression. Listen to the audio to get a sense of the rhythm and then cut loose!

Example 2f

Again, this would be a great time explore these triad shapes. Change the order of chords, rhythms, accents and mutes. See what you can come up with!

Using Suspended 2nds and 4ths in your progressions

If you're looking for some subtle tension to create a bit more movement in your chord sequences, look no further than suspended chords!

A "sus" chord is built by replacing a major or minor 3rd with a 2nd or 4th, which are named *sus2* or *sus4* chords respectively.

The neutral 2nd and 4th notes and the absence of a 3rd means that sus chords have less emotional definition. In fact, they're called suspended chords because these notes often want to resolve to a 3rd.

Let's learn the sus2 chords in the key of E Minor.

Example 2g

In the next example I have combined triads and power chords with our new friend the sus2 chord. The sus2 creates a momentary "hanging" tension before the power chord resolves it.

Example 2h

Using a combination of triads, power chords and sus2 chords, complete the unfinished chord progression below, replacing the dead notes with chord choices of your own.

Example 2i

At this point we've given suspended 2nd chords plenty of love, but what about sus4 chords? While having the same melodic neutrality as the sus2 (neither major nor minor), there's a different quality that suspended 4ths bring to the table.

Here are the diatonic chords of E Minor, this time with suspended 4ths.

Example 2j

In the next example lick, you'll play a combination of sus4 and triads to create a progression in E Minor that also has a few riffy elements. Be wary that the triad shapes I've used in this instance are different to the ones shown previously. The notes are the same, but the adjusted triad shapes work better with the sus4s.

Example 2k

Use the sus4 chord options from Example 2j, combined with the rhythms and riff styling above to create your own sus4 progression by completing bars three to eight with chords of your own choosing.

Example 2l

Using major and minor 6ths in your progressions

The 6th interval, whether major or minor, is a forgotten dark horse when it comes metal chord progressions. However, when used at the appropriate time, it can add tension or movement to make a chord sound flashy and interesting.

When playing these chords in drop tuning it's quite difficult to get the full triad and a 6th involved in one chord. The easiest way to incorporate the 6th is to substitute it where the 5th would be. For example, look at the formation of the E minor triad and Emb6 chord in drop tuning, shown below with fingerings.

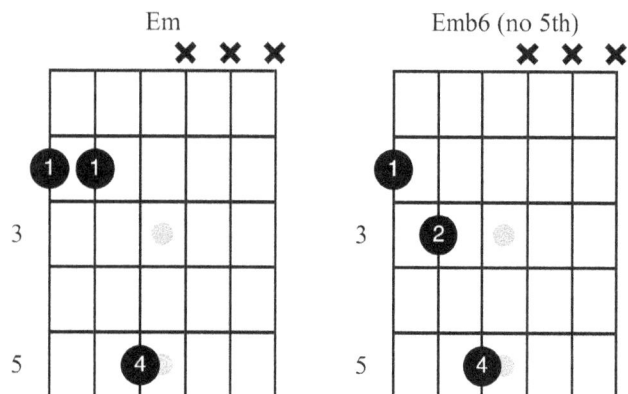

Play through the diatonic chords of A Minor using the drop tuning 6th shapes as shown below.

Example 2m

Here's a short progression in A Minor that uses 6th chords, triads and sus2 chords. Hear how the 6th chords are used in an interesting, melodic manner within the chord progression.

Example 2n

Now that we've found the diatonic 6th chords available in A Minor, play through the first bar of the example below, then complete the dead note bars with 6th chords of your choosing. Try having some fun blending the 6th chords with triads and sus2 chords.

Example 2o

As always, this is just the tip of the iceberg and you should know by now that this is your opportunity to get exploring. Replace different triads or power chords with 6th chords, change the rhythms, palm mute, use hammer-ons etc. Replacing just one or two chords will lead your ears to new creative places. Don't give up if you get stuck, keep working through any blocks.

Using major and minor 7ths in your progressions

As a younger man (yes, here comes a backstory), I'd listen to my older brother play and sing jazz standards. I was fascinated as to why there were so few barre or power chords and everything sounded so adult and polished. This "sonic adultness" (a term I just coined) came from the 7th chords used in so many of the songs he'd play AND, never in a million years did I think learning all the theory behind the construction and use of 7th chords would play a role in the way I write progressive rock and metal.

Play through the drop-tuned 7th chords in the key of F# Minor shown below. You'll be able to hear a level of sophistication and interesting colours that haven't been seen or heard in this book so far.

To play these chords comfortably in a drop tuning, I've omitted all major and minor 3rds from the chords. For example, when the first chord, F#m7 is played, the note order is F# (root), C# (5th) and E (minor 7th).

Example 2p

Next, play through this progression in the key of F# Minor using a combination of 7th chords, power chords and the occasional sus2.

Example 2q

Now, play through Example 2r, replacing all the dead notes with 7th chords or other chordal flavours of your own choosing.

Example 2r

One thing to keep in mind is that there are multiple formations and voicing of 7th chords. Below are the formations for 7th voicings in F# Minor, using the 5th, 4th and 3rd strings to play different voicings.

Example 2s

Using a combination of the voicings above created an example progression that shows all three possible voicings for a 7th chord. To mix things up, I've started the progression from a Dmaj7 chord to give the progression more of a D Lydian flavour.

Example 2t

Again, get creative. 7th chords are an acquired taste and you might want to use them sparingly in your writing. Or not! Go nuts!

Using octave chords in your progressions

For as long as I can remember, I've loved the sound of octave chords. From hearing them in the intro to *Cherub Rock* by Smashing Pumpkins, to the intense chorus of *Got the Life* by Korn, or how could we forget the soaring chromatic octaves in the very lengthy bridge of the Rage Against The Machine classic *Killing In The Name*. If my memory serves me correctly, this section of the song takes a firm stance on defying authority and is indeed riddled with swears. Naughty!

The magic of octaves is that they can take an otherwise simple melody and double it eight notes higher (or lower) to bring it to the forefront of a song. This is an opportunity to make it a real hook.

For starters let's play the D Natural Minor scale using octave chords as shown below.

Example 2u

Next, play through the octave scale in an ascending and descending manner.

Example 2v

In this exercise you'll play octave chords that work through the D Minor scale in 3rds. Playing these chords in a less linear manner gives an octave chord sequence more life and musicality.

Example 2w

Next, I've taken the octave chords and situations we've seen in the past three examples and paired them with a few power and suspended chords. This creates a cool amalgamation with a hooky and hummable melody.

Example 2x

Now move on to the next assignment. You'll use the same chordal ideas and timings but fill out the bars 2-8 with power chords and octave chord melodies of your own choosing.

Example 2y

See how many ideas you can come up with!

Creating arpeggiated riffs using chord progressions

An inventive chord progression can turn an otherwise good song into an amazing song. But once a nice set of chords have been selected, we don't necessarily have to resort to strumming them all the time. "What are the other options?" you ask. Well, let's find out.

Arpeggios are a great texture to enhance a chord progression instead of strumming.

When playing arpeggiated chords, I think it's best not to get too technical with the rhythms because the arpeggiated chord riff can tell enough of an interesting story without getting too intricate. If my chord progression has been carefully thought out, I don't feel the need to resort to interesting or "silly" rhythms to keep the listen engaged. However, my approach is not for everyone and should not be taken as gospel. At the end of the day, these are your songs and compositions, so it's really up to your preference and taste.

Arpeggiated chords can be played with either tight and tidy staccato or by letting the notes bleed together, depending on your preference. My general rule is that if the guitar is distorted, I'll use a staccato attack to arpeggiated the chord progression, but if the guitar setting is clean it can sound nice if the notes bleed together.

Let's take a simple chord progression and play through it with a strumming pattern as shown below.

Example 2z

Now that we've established a pleasant chord progression, play it in an arpeggiated manner. An excellent example of this approach is in the opening riff and verse of the Slipknot song *Dead Memories*.

Example 2z1

The approach above used ascending three-note groupings. In the next example we're going to do the complete opposite and descend.

Example 2z2

Another way to change the sound or approach of arpeggios is to double up each note. This means that the melodic content isn't too busy, but the rhythm has an element of speed. Riffs like this sound great when they are distorted and heavily muted by the picking hand.

Example 2z3

Finally, here's an arpeggiated approach created by varying subdivisions between the 1/8th and 1/16th notes. I've added different emphasis and altered the placement of the 1/16th notes. Bars one and two highlight the sixth string and emphasize the root note, while the 3rd and 4th bars highlight the 4th string to bring out the changing colours.

Example 2z4

Now you have a plethora of chordal material to work through. Try to write one progression for each section from scratch. Use different keys, scales and be as creative as you can within the parameters of the concept to really get the most out of it. When you feel you've grasped the concept and tested it enough, move on to the next idea.

As you get more confident, blend multiple ideas together. This could be something as simple as combining suspended chords with triads, and throwing octaves in between. You might shift between triads and 6th chords. There are no rules other than to keep combining options to see how they all work together.

Chapter Three – Creating Chordal Riffs

Sometimes I'll compose a single note riff that sounds great but when I go to record it, it sounds thinner than I wanted. A quick way to fatten it up, make it more melodic, or add some depth is to turn it into a chordal riff.

Here's some food for thought… Think about how "less fat" the verse of Metallica's *Master of Puppets* would be if, instead of power chords, it was played as single notes on the low E string. It's just not the same song! By using a power chord, the verse riff has extra grit and heaviness to it. However, the second riff of the song starting at 0:21 actually sounds amazing as a single note idea. The awareness of when to do one thing or another will make you a more versatile and interesting riff writer.

A good example of choosing a specific interval to create a chordal riff can be heard in AC/DC's *Rock and Roll Ain't Noise Pollution*. If we look at the intro/chorus riff, what makes it special is the harmonised major and minor 3rds added to the melody notes.

We could even add a dissonant interval like a b2, as used at 0:31 in the main riff of Children of Bodom's *Are You Dead Yet?* This approach really attacks the ears of the listener.

In this section we'll look at how to harmonise intervals to create chords so that when you are turning a single note riff into something chordal, you have an awareness of how the harmony sounds, and a procedure you can fall back on when you're writing.

Play through this chordal interval exercise that works its way through each chromatic interval from a b2 to the octave. This will help you hear what happens to a pedalled D note as the harmonised intervals change.

Example 3a

Below I've written my description of the feelings these intervals evoke when played together. They're a starting point for your own explorations, but do keep in mind that this is subjective, and their feelings are affected by what you play before and after each one – along with tempo, rhythm and a host of other things.

Chris Zoupa's Big List of Feelings (in D)

Interval	Note	Description
b2	Eb	Dissonant harmony, attacks listener (think Alfred Hitchcock's trademark *Psycho* music)
2	E	Suspended neutral sounding harmony, can be used as a quick deviation from the root note
b3	F	Minor 3rd, evokes sadness
3	F#	Major 3rd, evokes joy
4	G	Suspended neutral sound, similar emotional depth as the 2nd. Can be used as an inverse power chord or 5th interval
#4/b5	G#/Ab	Can be used as a bluesy b5 to create some tension in a minor context, but can also be used as a #4 to create some spacey dreamy tension in a Major / Lydian context
5	A	Power chord interval, little emotional content, but supports and thickens root note
b6	Bb	A sad interval but differs from the minor 3rd as it has tension and darkness to it. Can be used to pivot in and out of the 5th interval. See intro riff of Trivium's *Pull Harder on The Strings of Your Martyr* to hear this concept in context
6	B	A pleasant-sounding interval that can be used in a major or minor context. Can also be used to pivot in and out of the 5th interval. Listen to the verse of Chuck Berry's *Johnny B. Goode* to hear the interplay between the 5th and 6th interval
b7	C	Can be used in a major context to add a bluesy or flamenco flavour to a chord or riff, but can bring a jazzy funky vibe to a minor context
7	C#	Can create a pleasant tension with resolution from major 7th to octave or root in a major context. Can evoke a dark harmonic minor sound in a minor context which has somewhat of a Dracula or James Bond villain characteristic to it
Octave	D	Simply doubles root note one octave above. No emotions evoked. Adds power

I've created an exercise that turns these chords into a chuggy riff to help you hear these intervals in a more musical, metal context.

Example 3b

In the next example, I've only used notes from the D Minor scale. When these notes are harmonised, they create the following diatonic chords:

Dm | Emb5 | F | Gm | Am | Bb | C

The next exercise cycles through all of these diatonic chords, pairing them with their appropriate mode in one octave. The moving scales and droning root notes mean that every note of the scale now has a somewhat choral flavour.

Example 3c

Next, I've combined the two ideas above to create one unique riff. The implementation and inference of chord changes within this riff creates melodic interest and movement. I've also added in 1/16th notes to add galloping spurts of speed.

Example 3d

Now it's over to you.

I want you to use the concepts shown so far to create a riff of your own using the template below. Fill in the dead notes with your own chord changes and voicings.

Example 3e

Turning single note riffs into power chord riffs

I'd like to start the next section with a disclaimer, because I don't want to receive any hate mail. A single-note riff can be totally badass! I'm not knocking them at all, so don't "cancel" me just yet! They serve a great purpose. And, even if they're a little overused, most music lovers don't seem to mind.

However, playing devil's advocate, I'm going to tell you right now that you should explore how to break away from single note riffs and turn them into chord-based riffs.

As you now know, the 5th intervals contain very little emotion. That might sound like a red flag, but it actually means the 5th can be used to support and thicken any root note it's paired with. This makes it an obvious and easy candidate for helping to create chord-based riffs.

This concept is way easier than you might think.

To get started, let's look at a standard one-string, drop D, '90s grunge chug riff.

Example 3f

Let's use this as a building block to try the following idea.

This riff uses the same notes and fretboard positions but is played using flat-fingered power chords. I've added position variations on the fifth-string roots to show different ways to play the same notes and get different sounds.

For example, the C5 to D5 chord in bar four uses flat-fingered power chords on the 10th and 12th fret to create a more muffled, bass-heavy attack to the chords. As a result, these chords are more accentuated on the lower midrange frequencies. You can hear this idea in the flat-finger power chord riffs of Soundgarden's *Spoonman* or Smashing Pumpkins' *Jellybelly*.

On the flipside, the C5 to D5 in bar eight is played as sliding power chords on higher strings and lower on the fretboard. This will tend to accentuate the upper midrange frequencies of the chords. You can hear this in the main riffs of some Disturbed songs like *Indestructible* and *Stricken*.

Play through both four-bar variants of the riff to hear the different attack on the power chords.

Example 3g

C5 D5

P.M. P.M. P.M. P.M. P.M. P.M. P.M. P.M. P.M. P.M.

```
0—0—3—0—0—6—5—0    3—5—0—5—3—0—1—1    0—0—3—0—0—6—5—0    10—12—0—10—9—0—9—8
0—0—3—0—0—6—5—0    3—5—0—5—3—0—1—1    0—0—3—0—0—6—5—0    10—12—0—10—9—0—9—8
```

(position variant with slides)

C5 D5

P.M. P.M. P.M. P.M. P.M. P.M. P.M. P.M. P.M. P.M.

```
0—0—3—0—0—6—5—0    3—5—0—5—3—0—1—1    0—0—3—0—0—6—5—0    5—7—  5—4—  4—3
0—0—3—0—0—6—5—0    3—5—0—5—3—0—1—1    0—0—3—0—0—6—5—0    3—5—0—3—2—0—2—1
                                                                 0         0
```

Now that you have a brief understanding of how to turn a single-note riff into a power-chord riff, I want you to focus on creating some riffs of your own. To get you started, let's look at how to play power chords in D Minor.

The diatonic scale is repeated twice, first with the sixth and fifth string flat-finger chords and then with the fifth and fourth string variations.

Example 3h

Muffled lower mid frequencies

| D5 | E5(♭5) | F5 | G5 | A5 | B♭5 | C5 | D5 |

```
0————————1————————3————————5————————7————————8————————10————————12
0————————2————————3————————5————————7————————8————————10————————12
```

Clearer mid frequencies

| D5 | E5(♭5) | F5 | G5 | A5 | B♭5 | C5 | D5 |

```
0————————1————————3————————5————————2————————3————————5————————7
0————————2————————3————————5————————0————————1————————3————————5
```

56

Use straight 1/8th rhythms and the diatonic power chords to create a riff of your own using the template shown below. You're welcome to use either or regular flat-fingered power chords.

Example 3i

Now that we've explored how to turn a simple idea into mean and nasty power chord riff, let's look at how we could turn a simple metal-core riff into something chordal.

Here's a relatively simple hardcore chugged-metal riff using single notes. Play through it to get an understanding of the rhythm and melody.

Example 3j

Once you're comfortable with this riff in its single note state, we can start experimenting with chordal ideas.

With these chugs and scale notes, I've created a new riff using 3rds in D Minor to create a chord-based riff with a somewhat Iron Maiden/In Flames flavour.

Example 3k

Next, I harmonise the riff with 4ths and 5ths. These intervals can evoke different sounds and feelings. 4ths can sound glammy like Ratt or Motley Crue, but 5ths create more of an Anthrax or Disturbed vibe.

Have a play through Example 3l to get a feel for the kind of chordal riffs that can be created with 4th and 5th intervals.

Example 3l

Next, I want to show you how you can use a triad with an added 4th to create a riff. Here's a riff that takes influence from bands like Iron Maiden, In Flames, Trivium and Bullet For My Valentine.

Example 3m

The concept above is quite simple and predictable and definitely serves a purpose, but we can make it more interesting by adding in more rhythms and giving it more of a "chordal riff" sound.

Example 3n

Next, I've added in some string skips to access the 6th, 7th and octave intervals.

Example 3o

Testing harmonies for chord riff construction

We've now seen plenty of riffs based around the Natural Minor scale, so let's mix things up a bit! In the next example I've created a simple, chugged, D Phrygian Dominant riff that we'll use as a building block to create more chordal riffs later in this chapter.

Example 3p

Next, play through the D Phrygian Dominant scale in harmonised 3rds. Listen to the interplay between the 3rds, as this is how we'll turn our single note riff into a harmonised idea.

Example 3q

Here's that earlier riff harmonised in 3rds. I've added variations in the higher octave in the seventh and eighth bars, as often there are situations where different octaves of harmonies sound better.

Example 3r

Next, here's the D Phrygian Dominant scale in harmonised 4ths.

Example 3s

Now apply these intervals to our workhorse riff. Again, I've added variations in the seventh and eighth bars to show the options available to you in different registers.

Example 3t

Guess what?! Here's the Phrygian Dominant scale in 5ths! Learn it, then apply it to the riff in the following example.

Example 3u

Example 3v

Finally, we're going to look at how to play the D Phrygian Dominant scale in octaves.

Example 3w

This time you'll see that the melody played between the chugged notes is accentuated in octaves. By doubling up the same note in different registers, I accentuate the exotic evil melody. You can hear this concept being displayed perfectly in the introduction to Opeth's masterpiece *The Grand Conjuration*.

Example 3x

When Should One Riff Chordally?

Now you have explored these approaches, it might leave you in a bit of a pickle as to where to start. But not every time you write a riff using single notes does it need to be turned into something chordal.

For example, there's an amazing riff in Lamb of God's *Hourglass* that starts at 1:24. It begins as single notes then at 1:46 the entire riff is played as power chords. In this instance the riff goes from single notes to a chordal riff to make the heavy riff even heavier!

Another situation could be the main riff of Diamond Head's *Am I Evil*. I think I speak for all of us when I say that riff would sound terrible as a single note riff.

In the end, it's up to you. Experiment, think outside the box, and work through all the exercises and assignments shown in this chapter.

Chapter Four – Composing in Strange/Odd Meters

One of the coolest curve balls you can throw at your listener is to use unusual time signatures to add an interesting emphasis to your riffs. It creates an element of surprise, keeps the listener guessing and can give your music a point of difference. In a world full of chumps that only play songs in 4/4, you can be the one to stand tall and say, "No more!"

The quickest way to create this point of interest is to use odd meters in your compositions. In this chapter we'll look at 3/4, 5/4 and 7/8 time signatures (AKA the holy grail time signature of progressive rock).

Composing in 3/4

As far as uncommon time signatures go, 3/4 is quite rare in rock. 3/4 has been used in waltzes and traditional Celtic music for centuries. You might be saying to yourself, "Delightful Celtic music? That's sounds like a delightfully jolly time signature!" and you'd be half right, until you looked at 98.7% of every "church-burning" black metal song ever written.

3/4 can be used in any genre, you just need to figure out how you can make it work for you. To begin your 3/4 riff writing education, play through this evil riff in D Locrian. It will get you used to the feel of 3/4.

Example 4a

If you prefer a sound that's more technical, we can experiment with some more interesting rhythms.

This is still in 3/4, but this time I've varied between triplet 1/16th, and triplet 1/8th notes to create little bursts of fast gallops.

Example 4b

Using the rhythms from Example 4a, write a riff for bars one to four below. Bars five to eight use the rhythm from Example 4b. These two riffs could easily create two sections of a song.

Example 4c

In the next few examples, we'll explore some ways to approach composing chord progressions in 3/4. Our goals are to get used to the feel and strumming patterns, and to spawn some ideas for chord progressions of your own.

First, play through the progression below. You can hear this executed perfectly in the Opeth songs *Demon of the Fall* and *Ghost of Perdition*.

Example 4d

Next, you'll add more galloped rhythms to make the progression and rhythmic approach sound more complex. It's good to have ideas like this one in your toolbox as they are a less "draggy" than the progression above.

Example 4e

As a fun key-change idea, use triad shapes to compose a progression with the rhythmic timing of Example 4d.

Example 4f

The final idea I want to explore is to use arpeggiated riffs in 3/4. The first example uses two groups of three 1/8th notes per bar. One concept I like to use is to play the same root note over two bars but vary between triads and suspended chords.

Example 4g

Another arpeggiated variant you can use involves playing a six-note arpeggiated chord with four ascending and two descending notes. This approach is also used in the introduction to the Metallica classic, *Nothing Else Matters*.

Example 4h

Use the arpeggiated concepts from examples 4g and 4h to compose two arpeggiated chord riffs of your own in 3/4.

Composing in 5/8 and 5/4

5/8 and 5/4 time signatures have always fascinated me, as playing five beats per measure makes any melodic idea sound either tense or unfinished. You can often hear this time signature in movie scores, used to create tension or shortness of breath during high speed chase scenes, or fist fights above moving trains. It's most famously used in the *Mission Impossible* theme tune.

The interesting thing about 5/4 is that it can be super technical and poignant, as in Dave Brubeck's *Take Five* or the intro to Tool's *Vicarious*. The flipside is that it can also have a rock and roll "looseness", like in the main riff in the Soundgarden song *My Wave* or Queens of The Stone Age's *Hanging Tree*. How you use it is completely up to you.

To begin our journey down this odd time rabbit hole, play through this one-note riff in 5/8 that uses rests, 1/8th notes and 1/16th notes to create some interesting rhythms.

Example 4i

Next, I've composed a riff that uses similar timings with more notes to create melodic interest.

Example 4j

Using the rhythms from Example 4h and the melodic ideas from Example 4i, compose a 5/8 riff of your own, using the template below.

Example 4k

Here's a simple 5/8 chord progression in the key of F# Minor played in 1/8th notes.

Example 4l

The next example is written in 5/4 time signature using the D Lydian mode. The 5/4 signature means that each measure is twice as long as the 5/8 ideas above and there's significantly more time to play with different and interesting rhythms.

Example 4m

Using the rhythmic examples above, now write your own 5/8 and 5/4 progressions. A program like Guitar Pro can help you stay mathematically consistent when composing in complex time signatures.

While I'm a big advocate of actually playing your instrument, and think that people who compose their music *entirely* on Guitar Pro are doing themselves a musical disservice, in these early stages of composing and experimentation writing in Guitar Pro is super helpful.

Finally, let's look at some arpeggiated riffs in this F# Harmonic Minor Vicarious-style riff. The five beats are divided into accents of three, then two 1/8th notes. You can see how they are grouped in the example below.

Example 4n

Using this "three then two" division, try to create your own 5/4 riff using straight 1/8th notes in any key you like!

Composing in 7/8

Some of my favourite riffs and songs of all time are written in 7/4 or 7/8. Even as a young wee tot and way before I was a metal head, I thoroughly enjoyed Peter Gabriel's *Solsbury Hill* without realising the entire song was in 7/4. The main riff of the feel-good Foo Fighters classic *Times Like These* is also in 7/4.

However, 7/8 is also a staple of technical and progressive metal. Pink Floyd's *Money* and Led Zeppelin's *The Ocean* both somehow make 7/8 sound groovy and sexy. I also absolutely love the 7s in the verse of King Crimson's *Frame by Frame* at 1:07 – it's absolutely rad

As I grew older and discovered the charisma and social currency that comes with having a brooding demeanour, I found songs (that matched my pain) like *Them Bones* by Alice in Chains and *Deliverance* by Opeth – both of which are dark and "seveny" (a new word I just made up) and awesome.

Whatever your music tastes or level of brooding disposition, I think we can all agree that 7/8 is totally badass. With that in mind, let's look at Example 4o, which is a simple 7/8 riff, comprised entirely of 1/8th notes in D Minor.

Example 4o

In the next example I've created a more complex riff with changing subdivisions that drift between 1/16th notes and dotted 1/8th notes. This creates a rather technical and varied rhythm over the odd meter.

Example 4p

Having learned the two single note riffs in 7/8, create a riff of your own using the template below.

Example 4q

Now move on and play this chord progression in F# Minor using common rhythmic 7/8 strumming patterns.

Example 4r

Next, we'll explore another progression in F# Minor, but this time create interesting rhythms by introducing 1/16th notes. The addition of the faster subdivision adds an element of speed and technicality to the riff.

Example 4s

Use the two previous rhythm variations and the template below to create a 7/8 chord progression in the key of A Minor. First, here are the Am chords in Drop D tuning.

Example 4t

And here's your riff template!

Example 4u

Finally, let's look at a few ways to create arpeggiated riffs in 7/8.

Here's an arpeggiated concept that works in groups of four and three. This particular sequence is in A minor and I've used add9 chords across four strings.

Example 4v

Once you have a feel for a time signature playing straight 1/8th notes it's fun to mix it up by introducing 1/16th notes. This example combines multiple triads and sus2 chords, and shifts between 1/8th and 1/16th notes.

Example 4w

Use some of these rhythmic ideas to compose a 7/8 arpeggiated riff in any key or mode you like!

An Odd Conclusion

It's important to know how to compose riffs (whether they be single note or chordal) and full chord progressions in any time signature. However, a song's *structure* and your style shouldn't change too dramatically when playing in more obscure time signatures. The point of this chapter has been to give you options that broaden your horizons, *not* to drastically change the songwriter you already are.

"What now?" you ask!

Well, work through each section of this chapter again and do all the assignments. Experiment with the accompanying riffs and see if you can turn one little idea into a full song. I'm a firm believer in writing challenges and forcing myself to write. Not everything I write is gold and not everything makes it to an album… but that's OK guys! Song writing is a craft and needs to be treated as such. You have to make a few awful meals before you become a 5-star chef… so, get cookin'!

Chapter Five – Advanced Chords for Smart People

If you're the kind of composer that wants their chords and chord progressions to have more spice, then this section is where you'll learn some more advanced chord structures and sounds.

After composing a lot of songs, musicians sometimes find that predictable chords become something of a bore. This chapter will make sure you never get bored in your writing, and are ready to go from simple to complex and whacky.

Advanced chords can range from variations of add9s and 11s, to drop 2 and drop 3 voicings. I'll explain all of these as simply as possible, so that you're ready and prepared to rub your new-found smartness and chord education in some chump's face.

Composing with Add9 chords

Put simply, an add9 is the notes of a triad (root, 3rd and 5th) with an added 9th!

A Cadd9 chord is therefore a C Major triad plus the 9th: C (root), E (major 3rd), G (5th) and D (9th).

It sounds really cool in drop tunings if you order the notes 1, 5, 9, 3 from low to high. So, for an Fadd9 I'd play F (root), C (5th), G (9th) and A (major 3rd).

Using the 1593 formula, here are the diatonic add9 chords in drop D tuning.

Example 5a

This chord progression uses add9 chord and to make things more interesting and is played in 5/4.

Example 5b

Next, I've created an arpeggiated chord idea using add9s in the key of F Major, but I've also added time signature changes from 4/4 to 3/4 every second bar.

Example 5c

Composing with 7add11 chords

Say "minor 7 add 11" five times in a row as fast as you can. It won't teach you anything, but sometimes I think the complexity of a chord name can scare off the humble guitarist, so I want you to get comfortable saying it! As the name suggests the chord is a 7th chord with the addition of the 11th note of the scale. You can also think of the 11th as the 4th raised an octave.

The chord formula could be root, 3rd, 5th, 7th, 11th, but we often miss out notes like the 5th to make it playable on guitar.

If I wanted to create a Gmaj7add11 chord I'd need a root (G), a major 3rd (B), a 5th (D), a major 7th (F#) and an 11th (C#). I've found the best way to play these chords is root, 5th, 3rd, 11th and lastly the 7th.

Play through all the 7add11 diatonic chords in E minor using the 1-5-3-11-7 formula.

Example 5d

Having played through the 7add11 shapes move on to Example 5e, where I've created a chord progression in E Minor. This progression uses 7add11 chord shapes in 6/8 and will help you hear these chords in a more musical context.

Example 5e

Next, I've created an arpeggiated riff using 7add11 chord shapes over a 6/8 time signature This will help spawn some ideas as to how you can use 7add11 chords in arpeggiated riffs of your own.

Example 5f

Drop 3 (3157) voicings

You may have heard the terms "drop 2" or "drop 3" thrown around the cool-jazz-musician-smart-people community and thought to yourself, "Are they talking about music theory, or referring Mattel's card sensation Uno?!" They are not, in fact, talking about Uno, but a cool way to voice your chords.

To create a drop voicing we need a chord that contains four different notes, like a 7th chord.

I've said it once and I'll say it again, the guitar is a terribly designed instrument because it's normally stretchy and uncomfortable to play a "closed" voicing chord (voiced 1 3 5 7) and it doesn't always sound great either!

Try these closed 7th chord formations using C as the root note. Tricky, huh?

Example 5g

As you've probably found, these shapes are less than ideal. They also lack a quintessential rock or heavy metal sound, which makes them hard to use in rock and metal! To make these notes work, however, we can rearrange them and this is where drop 3 voicings are very helpful.

First, we have to establish which four notes are in our chord, then look at how we can rearrange them. Let's take a CMaj7 chord.

To create a drop 3 voicing of CMaj7, we simply drop the third voice from the top in a closed chord down an octave.

In a closed chord, the intervals are arranged, from high to low:

7th

5th

3rd

Root

By dropping the third voicing from the top down an octave (in this case the 3rd interval of the chord) we create the order

7th

5th

Root

3rd

The diagram below shows CMaj7 in closed voicing, then drop 3 voicing, and finally the same drop 3 voicing played in a lower octave (all in drop D tuning).

Example 5h

Now play through the diatonic chords of C Major using drop 3 voicings.

Sidenote: I've named the below "slash chords". No, not the Top Hat Rock God! The slash symbol gives the name of the chord to the left of the slash, and the bass note to the right of the slash.

For example, CMaj7/E means "Play a CMaj7 chord but make sure the E is in the bass".

Example 5i

I've created a simple progression with these chords. Play through Example 5j to hear these chords in a musical context and see if it spawns any ideas to create a drop 3 voicing progression of your own. Try playing earlier sequences with these voicings too!

Example 5j

Here's an arpeggiated riff using drop 3 chords in 7/8, so you can hear how they might sound in a prog rock, King Crimson-esque setting.

Try rearranging the signature to something straighter (or weirder) or change key when composing an arpeggiated drop 3 riff of your own.

Example 5k

Drop 2+4 (1537) voicings

The term "drop 2 and 4" is probably a bit less scary after the previous chapter, and creating a drop 2+4 voicing is a similar process to creating a drop 3. This time we drop the 2nd and 4th notes from the top of a closed position chord to create this spacious voicing.

A closed CMaj7 voicing organised,

7

5

3

1

Becomes,

3

5

1

7

Here's that process written out. First with an AMaj7 closed voicing, converted to a drop 2+4 voicing with an open string. The final voicing is the identical chord played with no open strings to create a movable shape in dropped tuning.

Example 5l

Now that we have a better understanding of drop 2+4 voicings in drop tuning, play through the diatonic chords of F# Minor using the shapes below.

To hear these voicings played in context with music, you can hear them in full effect in the chorus of the Periphery song *Flatline* at the 1:27 mark.

Example 5m

Here's a short chord progression so you can hear these chords in a more musical context. Try to write your own drop 2+4 voicing progression if this spurs any creativity in you. You can also change the key and time signature if you wish… there are no rules! Again, try playing earlier examples from this book (or any chord sequence you know) with these voicings.

Example 5n

Here's an arpeggiated riff with gallops and strums. As I've stated before, if any of these examples and ideas spur any creativity, please nurture it and see where it takes you!

Example 5o

In this chapter we've used some big words and made some big chords. In essence, we should be very proud of ourselves, but all this means *nothing* without application and experimentation.

I strongly suggest that you're sparing with your use of complex chords because it's all about context. There might be times a power chord or a simple triad is exactly what your song needs.

Go and write four progressions and four arpeggiated riffs based on add9s, 7add11s, drop 3s and drop 2+4 chords. Try using different signatures and keys outside your comfort zone. The purpose of this exercise is to really push the envelope of your creativity.

Go have fun and *go and make some music*!

Chapter Six – Bringing it All Together

In this final chapter I've composed a short song containing multiple ideas from this book to show how they could all intertwine to create a full piece.

It's worth mentioning that the song uses Drop D tuning and is mostly in D Aeolian with a few brief modulations to other keys.

Let's go through each section and examine the concepts used, and my compositional thought process.

Intro: Chordal Arpeggiations

An introduction is normally the calmest part of a song. With this in mind, I've used a clean guitar tone and arpeggiated various chord shapes in the key of D Minor. The aim is to create suspense and build into the distorted riff that occurs in the verse.

Verse A: Single Note Riff

This riff is based on a single string D Minor scale. I've used hammer-ons, pull-offs and rests to keep the riff interesting.

Verse B: Chordal Riff

The next riff uses the same motifs as Verse A but this time I've used power chords to turn the single note riff into a chordal riff. This develops the theme and gives it an extra layer of heaviness, as well as building the song up for the Pre-Chorus.

Pre-Chorus A: Scale-Based Riff in A Phrygian Dominant

To avoid my own composition getting tedious I added a key change to A Phrygian Dominant as well as using a chug riff based around the scale.

Pre-Chorus B: Scale Based Riff in D Phrygian Dominant

This riff is a continuation of the previous section, so the premise and writing techniques are the same. The most obvious change is that the key has shifted from A Phrygian Dominant to D Phrygian Dominant, which is the fifth mode of G Harmonic Minor.

Chorus: Chord Progression in G Minor

During the composition of Pre-Chorus B, I finished the riff on a brief Adim7 arpeggio. This arpeggio encourages another key change to G Aeolian for the chorus. Here I've used a repetitive dotted 1/8th note rhythm, as well as diatonic chords from G Minor. As far as the voicings go, I mostly use triads, suspended 2nd and suspended 4th chords.

Bridge: 7/8 Odd Time Signature Riff

In this bridge I've used the D Dorian scale as I felt the listener has heard enough Aeolian and Phrygian Dominant by now. I also use the 7/8 time signature and directly ripped off the timing of King Crimson's *Frame by Frame*.

Outro: 7/8 Odd Time Signature Chords

I wanted to end with a heavier vibe, so I brought back some chunky chords with a disgusting tritone chord. Once again, the 7/8 time signature creates a feeling of shortness of breath and it's delivery ends the song with a surprising bang.

Combine these ideas in your own writing and see how much mischief you can get up to!

Have fun!

C.Z. 2021

Fundamentally Insane

Example 6a – Clean guitar backing part

Example 6b – Fundamentally Insane

Intro - Chordal Arpeggiations

Verse A - Single Note Riff

Verse B - Chordal Riff

Pre-Chorus A - Scale Based Riff A Phrygian Dominant

Pre-Chorus B - Scale Based Riff D Phrygian Dominant

Chorus - Chord Progression in G Minor

Bridge - 7/8 Odd Time Signature Riff

Outro - 7/8 Odd Time Signature Chords